POEMS BY
JULIA
ZWAYNE

ALL THINGS
BROKEN &

BEAUTIFUL

What if pain was not forever?

Bridge-Logos, Inc.

Newberry, FL 32669

All Things Broken & Beautiful by Julia Zwayne

Copyright© 2025 by Julia Zwayne

Printed in the United States of America.

Library of Congress Control Number: 2025937159

International Standard Book Number: 978-1-61036-918-3

Interior Layout and Cover Design:
Ashley Morgan | GraphicGardenLLC@gmail.com

VP 9/25

To my parents, E.Z. and Rachel.

———————

Thank you for loving me with an unwavering love,
and for holding me close in my brokenness.

CONTENTS

INTRODUCTION

I often wonder what would happen to the human soul if all that weighed upon it had no release, no escape. Would we simply cease to exist, thrust into the ocean of our agony with no way to bear such a weight? What a gift it is that we are not meant to restrain our lamenting, to imprison our pain within us. Our Father has given us the freedom to pour forth our complaints, our deepest of sorrows. Look upon the blended colors of a canvas, flip through the pages of a tear-stained journal, listen to the haunting notes of a heart-wrenching song, peer into the lines of a lamenting poem. There you will find pain and brokenness that has been channeled into the finest forms of art, the truest displays of beauty. Best of all, our most excruciating of heartaches can be offered in prayers straight to the Lord's ears.

I like to think of my poems as prayers that find their way to truth. When I begin to write, it feels as if the blackness within is pouring straight from my pen, and I hardly know what I'm writing. All I know is that He is listening. As you will see when you turn these next pages, each of my poems collapses into the arms of truth and comfort, even if the journey feels as if I have been crawling toward a tiny glimmer of light.

Dear reader, I pray that these poems will quiet you with the gentle reminder that you are not alone in your pain. When you read the darkness in these pages, I hope that you will search for the light that whispers in the brokenness. I pray that when you close this book and lay it to rest, hope has shouted at you as you accompanied me through the deep valleys. Every piece of poetry in this collection comes from the scribblings of a broken human—the pleading prayers of one who has sat in the rubble of heartache. If you should walk away with one truth, let it be this: all that is broken is made beautiful in the end. Remember who holds you in the darkness. Pain is not forever, my friend. May you cling to the Restorer of our souls.

Part One

THE MESS

BROKEN

Heal the broken parts of me
That still lay tender beneath
The tumbling chaos of existence.
Restore the shattered pieces
That hide under
The dust of suppression
And the clutter of self-protection.
Please mend the tattered corners of my soul,
That I may breathe freely again,
And walk in Your glorious peace.
I search for the key
That locks me in this prison of brokenness,
Only to find it clasped tightly in a hand that is
   my own.
Wholeness and healing
Breathe upon my face;
They are so very near.
I must simply run forward
Into the arms of Him who will lavish me
With these gifts I so deeply desire.

THE STORM OF THE HEART

When fierce and ragged winds descend
Upon the ocean blue,
I tremble when I watch the waves
That tumble, crash, and spew.
The sky becomes an angry grey,
The clouds begin to weep,
A storm of terror falls with force,
And ends the ocean's sleep.
This is not the beach's shore,
Or somewhere on the coast,
I've given you a tiny glimpse
Of something I fear most.
The chambers of my trembling heart
Are filled with crashing waves
And restless winds that tear me up,
That throttle hope that saves.
If you have battled with these gales
Of sin and doubt and fear,
Remember that the storms at sea
Must always disappear.
The ocean of the darkest night
Of which you know quite well
Can seem a total stranger

When it doesn't seethe and swell.
The God who reigns above these storms,
Can calm them with a word,
And we must trust that morning's light
Will show our prayers were heard.
Your tumbling heart may tear you down,
And cause you to despair,
But when the sun breaks through the clouds,
You'll know that He was there.
Cling tightly to the boat of trust,
Through crashing waves of pain,
Then rest upon His peaceful sea,
As sunshine soothes the rain.

SACRED PATH

I've walked along the shore of Doubt,
I've climbed the cliffs of Dread,
I've stumbled into pits of Fear,
When Hope was all but dead.
I've crawled through valleys of Regret,
Through deserts of Despair,
I've waded through the swamps of Pain,
And Sorrow's tangled snare.
I've scaled the mountains of my Shame,
Crossed rivers full of Grief,
I've slept in trees of Idleness,
Attached there like a leaf.
I've hidden in the caves of Spite,
With Envy by my side,
I've crossed the plains of Loneliness,
And climbed the hills of Pride.
Dissatisfaction, dark and cold,
Has lashed me with its waves,
Bitterness became my chains,
And I, one of its slaves.
I've crashed through thorns of Disrespect,
Through gales of stark Defeat,
Temptation has consumed me

Sacred Path

In a storm of snow and sleet.
I've plunged myself in Selfishness;
A lake I just can't leave,
The hurricane of deep Distress
Has left me much to grieve.
Indifference has enclosed my form
In shadows dark and deep,
The pelting rain of Anger and Rage,
Has robbed me of my sleep.
Each cavern, plain, and rugged cliff,
Each ocean, lake, and stream,
Each stumble, fall, and grave defeat,
Each pain-filled, strangled scream,
Has drowned me in a blackened sea,
Has led me to my doom,
Has snuffed out every beam of light
And enclosed me in a tomb.
But wait, this map of deep despair,
So stained with blood and tears,
Is somehow mixed with something more
Than sins and pain and fears.
This journey was a sacred path
Into the dark unknown,
Led gently by a mangled hand
To kneel before a throne.
The blackened sin inside my heart

Had pierced and maimed and slain
The One who saw my every fall
Through snow and sleet and rain.
Perhaps this journey brought me low,
So He could lift me high,
Drowned me in the deepest fear,
That He would hear my cry.
My sin will never dissipate,
Nor leave my quaking heart,
But now I know He's always there,
My fortress from the start.
Forgiveness, oh how sweet it is,
His mercy cloaks my frame,
When wails of pain consume my heart,
I'll call upon His name.

YOU ARE WITH ME

Lord, You are drawing me closer,
Oh so gently,
Oh so quietly.
When my eyes are heavy with tears,
When my heart can't handle another blow,
When the silent wails of my soul pierce the night,
Your nearness smothers the pain.
I am drowning in Your presence,
Sinking into Your warm embrace.
When my grief is blinding,
I will look at You
I will gaze at Your beauty
Until my eyes sting
And I can see nothing else.
When I look to my right,
When I look to my left,
You are there.
I can't see the darkness anymore
Nor does the pain grasp me with cold fingers.
You chase my fear and sadness
To the far corners of the earth.
You are with me,
You are with me,
You are with me.

HIS BOTTLE OF TEARS

A torrent—raging, ever pouring,
Through the night,
And daytime's sight,
Seldom gentle; mostly roaring,
Such a fight,
Without much light.
My tears are raindrops in this cyclone,
Here I cry,
And deeply sigh,
It feels so dark; I'm so alone,
My cloudy sky
Will not run dry.
And yet a dream, a distant star,
A dream that's swept
Through nights I've slept,
Depicts a sacred, crystal jar,
In which are kept
The tears I've wept.
This bottle's always filled with liquid,
Struggle shows
As sorrow grows,
But even when I've felt I've drifted,
Jesus knows

Each tear that flows.
He keeps this bottle in His care,
It fills and fills,
But never spills,
He hears each trembling, pleading prayer,
He comes and stills,
My fears and thrills.
I've wandered often, far and near,
Each step I took,
Is in His book,
And at each dripping, flowing tear
That fills my brook,
He stops to look.

TO THE GIRL WITH THE BROKEN HEART

Your thoughts are like a black cavern;
Bleak, empty, and dark.
And yet out of this cavern
Erupt vibrant memories
Of giddy laughter; breathless moments
Full of wonder and romance.
As fast as they come, they disappear;
And there you are, staring out of a window
As raindrops trickle down the glass
Like the tears on your cheeks.
You inhale rejection
And exhale loneliness;
You fog the glass with your misery,
As the gloom outside
Laughs in your face.
But you're fine.
You're "doing great."
You're "just busy with school and work
But other than that,
Doing well."
You're happy,
You're "moving on."

To the Girl With the Broken Heart

"You're over him, right?" they ask.
"You don't think about him every day
Like you used to, right?"
You smile, but you know full well
That your heart is fragile,
And is on the verge
Of shattering again.
You pray for the pain to vanish,
You wonder if you'll ever
Wake up without a storm of tears
Clouding the horizon of your eyelids.
You wonder if you'll ever
Stop caring
About what he thinks of you.
His last words that ended everything
Echo in your ears
A thousand times.
They are deafening,
Like gunshots in the still night air.
You relive every moment
Like rewinding a movie
Over and over;
You study each scene,
You wonder at what moment
You slipped up
And ruined everything.

Several different emotions
Run through you
Like debilitating viruses
Back to back,
Leaving you weak and exhausted.
One moment you can't stand
The thought of him,
And the next,
You long to be with him again.
When you run into him
You are torn between
Pride and vulnerability.
You want him to think
That life is great without him;
You want to make him jealous.
And yet,
You want him to know
How much he's hurt you
And how broken you are.
You want him to be sorry.
Both of these thoughts
Torment your mind
And cause you to wallow
In your tears and misery.
…
Time passes.

To the Girl With the Broken Heart

You still cry,
You still find yourself slipping
Into moments of gloom and loneliness.
But ever so slowly,
You begin to realize
That letting go
And turning to Someone else
Is the only answer.
As soon as you loosen your grip
And surrender it all,
You begin to heal.
Your emotions are no longer
Bound to one human being
And controlled by him.
The claws that ripped at your heart
Give up when they find
That they cannot hurt you anymore.
When you give your heart
To the One who made it,
You find that nothing else
Has power over it any longer.
Instead of screaming at the night,
You lie there quietly,
Filled with the presence
Of your Protector and Healer.
You may not hear His voice;

You may not feel rescued,
But you know He is there.
In fact, your brokenness
Is what sent you running
To Him in the first place.
This is a gift.
He is more precious than any fairy tale,
Any rush of butterflies,
Any blissful romance.
You may tell yourself
That you are not enough.
You're not.
Only Christ is enough,
And He is the One
In whom you find your identity.
The love a man can lavish
Upon you
Is filth and rubbish
Compared to the love
Christ showers you with
Every
Single
Day.
Your heart may still be broken,
But the One who holds it
Is not.

To the Girl With the Broken Heart

When the torrents of rain
Drench and threaten to drown you,
Remember that Divine storms
Water the tender soil of your heart
To produce blooming buds of joy.
He is a faithful gardener
And He loves your heart
With a terrifying love.
You cannot comprehend it.
The girl with the broken heart
Is me.
And I hope she's listening.

THE BROKEN ROAD

The aching is relentless,
Like a hammer being thrown
Against a gong,
Over and over.
I wish the pain would magically vanish,
And I could move on with life,
As if nothing had happened.
But I've been on this path before,
And I know that healing and comfort
Steal softly into the room,
Soothing the heart with a subtle gentleness
When you least expect it.
His love is near and ready
To descend upon me
When pain cripples my soul.
Oh how I long for joy
To burst inside of me again.
While I wait for its soft murmur,
I will cling to the rock of hope
As the waves of affliction batter and bruise me.
It will soon pass,
For violent storms do not last forever.

YOU SEE ME

You see me
When I hide beneath the covers
And soak my pillow with tears.
You see me
When my heart trembles,
And every step I take is labored.
You see me
When I crumble beneath fear
And drown in failure.
You see me
When I lay alone in the darkness
And listen to the ramblings of my mind.
You see me
When I allow the weight of the world
To crush me into a state of paralysis.
You see me
When pain clutches my soul
With its iron claw.
You see me
When darkness caresses me
With its frigid fingers
And envelops me in an embrace of despair.
You see me

When I dwell on the words of others,
And pick them apart long after they've been said.
You see me
When I try to tend to my wounds on my own,
And no one else is aware of my suffering.
You see me
When everything in me is weary,
And I barely have the strength to pray.
My struggles do not go unnoticed,
Nor is one tear forgotten.
I forget that you sit beside me
On those sleepless nights
And hold my fractured heart together.
You are an attentive, observant God,
Who remembers
Every one of my painful moments.
Thank You for seeing me
When I feel invisible.
You are more beautiful
Than anything this world may display.
Help me to see Your beauty
In every waking moment,
In every dawning day.
Help me to remember
That every breath I take
Is a reminder of Your grace and goodness.
This is beauty magnified.

THE CONDUCTOR

So many people,
And yet I see none of their faces;
They are walking shells
As I push myself through the masses,
Through this place I've been before,
This place of swirling smoke, sputtering engines,
Piercing whistles and sweat-soaked
    bustling bodies.
The stones beneath my feet are utterly hollow
As my heels click against them
With both urgency and hesitancy.
I am at the dreaded platform
Gazing down at the steel tracks,
Filled with thoughts of madness,
A dizzying urge to throw myself upon the tracks
Instead of departing on the train that is coming to
    claim me.
And then I hear it:
The monstrous chugging,
The deafening whistle, like a wail piercing the air,
The curtain of smoke, swallowing me,
    drowning me,
The leviathan on wheels, barreling toward me in all
    its black terror.

It sputters sparks as it finally comes
To a screeching halt.
The bodies around me shrink back;
Each person falls away as the smoke curls
  around me.
The wailing in my ears comes from
  somewhere within
As all chatter around me is silenced.
It is only I on the platform,
Staring at the metal beast in front of me.
I take one step forward
But I cannot board it —
I will not.
Not this time.
Before I can retreat from the tracks,
Before I can vanish into the crowd,
One of the doors flies open
And I am being grasped by my wrists,
By my arms,
By several hands.
I cannot see their faces,
But I am pulled from the platform,
Thrust into the train,
And pushed into a car by myself
As the train lurches forward
And the station passes by my window in a blur.
My breath fogs the window
As sobs escape me,

As I am ripped away from all that is dear to me.
My world,
In all its bliss, comfort, and familiarity
Is gone.
I sit in the static silence,
Not daring to look out the window,
Wasting away in my grief and loneliness,
Shriveling in this vehicle of pain.
I've been on these tracks before;
I've been claimed against my will,
Thrown into this misery I have no control over.
Suddenly, something catches my eye;
I look up, and before me is the most
Beautiful sight I've ever seen.
A world of green –
Startlingly vibrant, rolling hills,
Streams of glassy water,
A carpet of color-splashed flowers.
I move toward the window
In awe of the sight before me.
There is a knock behind me,
And the door of my train car
Slides open.
An old man stands just outside the door
Holding onto a cart filled with refreshments.
"Anything to drink, my dear?" he asks.
"Some water, please," I say quietly.
As he hands me a cup, I ask,

"Sir, where are we headed?"
The old man smiles.
"That is up to the conductor," he says.
"This train does not stop until
He is satisfied with the journey.
But take heart, my dear.
The trip is as beautiful as it is dreadful.
And when it is over,
This train will bring you home again."
I turn to look out the window once more,
And it all comes flooding back to me.
The journeys I had been on before –
The loneliness, the sorrow, the fear of the unknown.
But I remember the beauty,
The hills, the rivers, the waterfalls, the mountains.
After each trip, I was never quite the same.
What I remembered the most was this:
The conductor always brought me home.
"Is there anything else you need?" the old man asks,
Interrupting my thoughts.
"No, sir," I say, relaxing in my seat.
"I'll be alright.
I've been here before."
The old man leaves me
Sitting in this lonely car,
In this monstrous train called Pain.

The Conductor

But perhaps without it—
Without this vehicle I know so well,
I would not know the heart of the conductor,
The one who I know will bring me home.

BLACK STALLION

I wish I could bridle this dark horse in my soul;
I grip reigns that cut into my skin and pull with all
   the strength I have.
Hooves trample my insides,
As this black steed rips through the deep recesses
   within me.
I am always straining,
Gasping,
Fighting,
To hide this beast inside.
The harder I smother him,
The more violently he resists me.
Shall I whip him into submission?
Shall I break him until he is tame?
I strive to pull him inside,
To bar him behind a fence he cannot escape,
And wait until his lathered sides stop heaving,
And his wild eyes lose their terror.
But he is easily spooked;
This mighty stallion does not know his own strength.
With hooves of steel
And a fire in his bosom,
He thrashes and tramples all in his path.

Black Stallion

Perhaps I am too hard on him—
Yet I can hardly bear his wild nature,
And the havoc he wreaks every waking moment.
I am afraid of him now;
I choke on the wake of dust he leaves behind him,
I hide when his piercing whinny rents the air,
I try to stay out of his way, but I can't seem to escape.
I tremble in a cloud of dust,
Then, with the sound of hoofbeats echoing
   all around me,
I hear a soft voice linger in the air.
The pounding steps are suddenly a gentle patter;
The whinny of terror fades to a soft whimper,
As the dust settles and the chaos is stilled.
A quietness descends over my soul.
No longer is this dark horse reigning with terror,
Nor is he galloping around in confusion.
Someone else has tamed him,
Has let him wander the pasture of my soul
And graze quietly in the field.
The great horse Master,
The tamer of pain,
Has taken my turmoil and broken its wild nature.
This Master has not broken its spirit,
For the beast still roams about inside me,
Kicking up dust in the dark moments,

Occasionally spooked by the piercing memories.
But this steed is tame,
Filled with peace.
Perhaps I can ride this stallion,
And softly canter through the pastures of my soul,
To see the beauty in the midst of distress.
When he flies into a rage again,
When he thrashes my heart in a moment of distress,
I will run to his Master
And He will rescue me,
For He is my Master too.
I cannot be rid of this dark horse of pain,
Nor can I break his spirit,
Nor temper his wild soul.
But now that I know his true Master,
Perhaps I can call him friend.

COBWEBS

Tumbling,
Always tumbling.
Falling through my nightmarish thoughts
Into a never-ending chasm
Of oblivion.
These thoughts
Stick to my flesh like giant spider webs,
Tangling me in their suffocating mass,
Wrapping me in a cocoon of imprisonment.
It takes one tumble,
And I'm free-falling with no escape.
Why does this keep happening?
Why can't I gain control?
I'm sorry, Lord.
I'm sorry.
Please rescue me from my self-inflicted torment.
Catch me in Your net
Of truth,
Because I can't seem
To stop falling through these cobwebs
Of lies.

BEAST

This world is a kaleidoscope of color,
A dazzling, swirling mess of tantalizing happiness,
A soft haze of rosy opportunity,
A deafening concert of exhilaration.
You are lulled by its comforting words,
You are seduced by its beauty,
You are thrilled by its flashing lights,
You are beckoned by its offer of everlasting
    fulfillment.
You rush into its arms,
Expecting pleasure, security, happiness,
But the rosiness fades,
The flashing colors
Are smothered in darkness.
The thrill in your veins turns icy with fear,
And the arms that welcomed you
Begin to suffocate you
As everything crumbles
And disintegrates around you.
A façade,
A lie,
A projection of fantasy,
A nonexistent reality.
That's all it ever was.

Beast

Its delicacies turn to ash in your mouth,
The exhilarating music fades to harsh silence.
You scream into the void
That sucks away every particle of light.
You back against a wall
As the darkness curls toward you
With gnarled fingers,
Beckoning you
Into its depths.
The previous glories
Have transformed into a beast of terror.
Why have you fallen in love with such a traitor?
Why have you surrendered your trust so blindly?
Is it because you see yourself
In that alluring mess?
The dazzling sparkles that drew you in
Are merely flashes of your own reflection.
The beckoning voice you heard is yourself,
Calling you to partake
In self-gratifying pleasure.
You ran quickly,
For you could not be parted
From the love of your life.
The dark beast who lashes out at you is not the world
After all.
It is a monster
Who shares your name.

PERFECT LOVE

We were acquainted when I was small;
I met you when I cowered beneath the tangled
    sheets of my bed and cried out in the night.
You grabbed me in your choking grasp;
You drained the life out of me,
And yet I clung to you.
I invited you back again
At my weakest moments;
I hated you, but I loved you.
You told me to embrace the darkness and flee
    from the light.
I shuddered when you held me,
But you were the easiest to run to,
And you never wanted to leave me.
The more I clung to you,
The more I became dependent on you.
I could have sent you away,
I could have chased you into the shadows,
But you lurked near me at every moment,
And fed off of my despair.
When my days were filled with sunshine,
You appeared unannounced,
And shut the blinds tight

Until every beam of light was blotted out.
I told myself I wouldn't let you destroy the plans
  I made,
And I wouldn't allow you to throw my joy into
  the fire.
But I continued to welcome
Your words that tore up my insides;
The lies that put me in shackles.
I watched my hope go up in flames.
One day, you knocked on my door, but I didn't answer.
I sat there,
Waiting to see what you would do.
You knocked and knocked
But didn't try to come in.
I put my face to the crack of the door,
Telling you to leave.
"Why?" you hissed, "You need me."
There was a moment of silence.
You knocked again, but I kept the door shut.
"If you want to come in here so badly, why don't you
  force your way in?"
You laughed. "I can't come in, unless you let me.
You have always invited me willingly.
Why do you resist me now?"
"There is someone else who takes care of me," I said.
"He doesn't shut the blinds,

Nor does he suffocate me in darkness,

Nor does he laugh at my suffering.

My new protector keeps me safe."

Your footsteps were hollow as you walked away.

I no longer heard your rasping voice at my door,

But I knew you had not disappeared completely.

There were times when I caught a glimpse of you
    in the street.

You tried to call out to me,

But I hurried away, knowing I could never return.

"Who is he?" I turned slowly as your chilling wail
    pierced the air.

"His name is Love," I declared.

"And he has replaced you.

For perfect love casts out Fear."

GOODBYE

Some goodbyes are not by choice.
When a loved one's soul leaves this earth,
One must part with that person
And say a gut-wrenching farewell
With a pain that is indescribable.
However,
Some goodbyes are a choice.
There are those who leave your life,
Who may abandon you with selfish intentions,
Or walk away in a state of indifference.
Those people have already said farewell,
And yet it's possible for you to not say it back,
To refuse to shut that door with a click of finality.
You keep them close to your heart,
You lock them away so they won't escape,
So you can relive the happy times you had with them.
You refuse to say goodbye,
Because if you do,
You are walking away from your last memory
Of happiness, familiarity, and comfort.
You don't want to walk into unfamiliar territory,
You don't want to let your heart out of its cage again.

You gave your heart away already.
Why not let this person keep it?
But you are miserable;
You are far from free.

SHAMELESS TEARS

Tears are consuming;
They flood, they drown, they burn.
There is no escape from them,
There is no relief from them.
I wipe them away,
I try to hold them in,
But they keep returning with a vengeance.
Why do they visit me when no one is near to
 comfort me?
Why do they strike in the dark and lonely hours?
Why do they emerge as soon as the happy moments
 are over?
I hate my tears.
They leave me weak and vulnerable.
And yet
Somehow
They are my friends.
If tears were so formidable,
Why does my Father collect them?
If tears were so shameful,
Why does God welcome them?
Without tears, my heart would be hard,
Calloused, stony.

My tears create a lens of compassion,
An awakened experience that draws me to the pain
   of others.
The more I cry for my own hurts,
The more I cry with others.
The floodgates open when I see
The tears stream down another's face.
If tears will keep me humble,
If they will keep me on my knees,
If they will release my pain
And keep me from bitterness,
Then I will welcome them with open arms.
I will not bottle them up,
For my Father will keep them in a bottle of His own.

DUST COLLECTOR

I want to know
Why I shroud the cloudless vibrancy of my world
With the fog of hypothetical terrors.
Explain to this miserable soul
Why all things beautiful
Are trampled by the feet of my wandering thoughts.
Am I on a witch hunt
For things that do not exist?
I dump water
On the peaceful fire that is my life
To obliterate any chance of mass destruction.
And then I wonder why I'm so terribly cold.
You must stop this.
You must run with joy into the wings of a
    glorious morning
And shout with the strong lungs within you.
Sing with the birds,
For it is a miracle that your eyes beheld another day.
Your Maker is not gifting you
With wrapped presents full of empty air.
The sweet surprises you encounter
Are not mirages to madden your mind.
Embrace these daily joys!

Stop choosing to sit in the dusty closet of your
   ever-chattering mind,
But choose freedom.
Yes, He may bring the blessings
For a mere season,
But if you do not accept them now,
They will only collect dust
Beneath the weight of your own fear,
And then vanish forever.
Do not offend the Giver,
For He is the only one
Who can truly give good gifts.
I am swimming in lies,
And I scream for help
As the water closes over my head.
Why did I jump into these frigid waters?
Did I truly believe this would protect me
From disappointment?
I run away from dashed hopes
Only to crash into the arms
Of paralyzing anxiety.
This is not what God wants for me.
Every golden sunrise,
Every gloomy storm
Is a reason to have communion with my Father.

Dust Collector

Be it praise or lament,
I will raise my voice to magnify the Giver.
I will not destroy what He has made perfect.

PAIN

Pain.
It lies beside me each night,
It greets me with a kiss each morning,
It holds my hand with cold fingers
And follows me around all day.
But what is pain?

Pain is a prison with bars of steel.
Once you are within its walls of stone,
You are faced with a life-sentence.

Pain is a disease.
It eats you away from the inside out;
Its presence causes others to flee,
Leaving you in its isolating agony.

Pain is a fire that never stops burning.
It ravages and sears your flesh,
But you are never fully consumed,
Leaving the fire to burn and burn.
That is pain.
At least that is what pain feels like.

But—

Pain

What if pain
Was a rock hitting the surface of a glassy lake?
The initial impact causes a ripple of damage
That reaches far and wide,
The peace of the lake being disrupted for a time.
But ever so slowly and gently,
The ripples become smaller,
And the rolling water smooths into a calm body
  once more.
The rock finds its place at the bottom of the lake,
And all is tranquil on the surface once more.

What if pain was a surgeon's knife?
It cuts deep into the flesh,
Producing an excruciating, maddening sensation.
Relief seems impossible,
Any good outcome a ridiculous notion.
But once the work is done,
And the flesh is stitched up neatly,
The healing will begin.
The storm of pain settles,
And will be better than before.

What if pain was a winter storm?
It attacks the land with frigid fury,
Covering all life in layers of snow and ice,

Killing all that is green and beautiful.
No one can stand in its wake;
It slashes and pierces and rages.
But soon it will exhaust its anger,
And all is beautifully white and silent.
The land is blanketed by a protective layer of
    glowing ivory.
Soon the frosty layer will melt,
And all will be startling green once more.

What if pain was not forever?
What if it came in crashing waves, but retreated
    when chased by the peace of God?
What if pain ushered us into a heavenly presence?
What if pain was essential to the Christian walk?
Oh, how pain is a mere blip
On the horizon of eternity.
Perhaps pain is God's tool of rescue;
A rope to pull us away from ourselves
And onto the shore of His goodness.
I will not pretend to welcome it,
But while it sits beside me in this dark room,
I will open the shutters,
Drinking in the light of His presence
Until the grip of pain's hand loosens from mine,
And it slips quietly from the room.

Part Two

THE MIRROR

EMPTY SHELL

I look at her with curiosity
And she gazes back at me,
Her eyes empty and hollow,
Her face pale and spent.
Her features are shrouded in sadness,
Her body sags with fatigue,
And though she doesn't speak,
Her eyes cry out for help,
Begging me to rescue her from her misery.
She is a shell of the woman she was,
A shell of who she wants to be.
Her hair is in place
And she has taken time to put on makeup,
But nothing can cover or mask her suffering.
I wish I could help her,
But I know it is impossible.
And yet—
I know another who can.
Someone who will hold her sorrowful heart
While she tries to face the world.
Someone who will sit beside her
When she cries in the night.
Someone who will mend her

And restore her again.
I know she knows this.
I look at her once more,
Taking in the deep sorrow before me.
I step away from the mirror,
Knowing that one day
I will return to see
Not an empty shell,
But a different woman altogether.

YOU LOOKED ON ME

You gave me everything,
You held nothing back from me;
You gifted me with life itself.
I never thanked You once—
I threw Your gifts into the dirt,
And ran away from Your love.
I dove headlong into the swirling mass
Of my own desires.
I chased after every illusion,
I slandered Your name,
I defied You with my words,
My actions,
My very life.
Coated in my own filth,
I wandered the streets of loneliness,
Stumbled through the gates of destruction,
And fell into the arms of depravity.
I hid from everything;
From those who loved me,
From my own reflection,
From You.
I felt nothing;
I lay like a corpse in my own misery,

Then one day,
I heard You coming,
I cried out in panic
And tried to hide my filthy rags,
Tried to conceal my fallen state.
I half-expected You to pass me by,
For I was repulsive in every way.
Instead, You stopped to look at me.
I could not meet Your gaze,
For my weak and wretched condition
Was self-inflicted and horrifying to look upon.
You bent down and gathered me in your arms;
You pulled me from the mud
And carried me home.
I marveled at Your kindness.
I wondered why someone as holy as You,
As spotless and pure,
Would even look upon me,
Much less touch me.
I never would have run to You on my own,
Nor crawled out of the pit,
Unless You had rescued me.
It was by Your grace
That my rags are now sparkling white and spotless.

BLANK SPACES

What do I do with grey?
Why is there pain in the blank spaces?
I see nothing
But I feel everything.
The clock is ticking,
Ticking,
Ticking,
But I stand between time and space
As the world spirals around me in dizzying circles
    of warped images and distorted faces.
I'm hurtling forward at 100 miles per hour
And yet nothing has changed.
I hear the drip, drip, dripping of my own thoughts;
They fill my brain until it is almost bursting at
    the seams.
I try to gather them up,
But they sift through my fingers like sand.
They escape me, they flee as I chase their
    chaotic bickering.
I am full, I am vibrant, I am strong,
I am empty, I am muted, I am weak.
I am brittle bones, I am nothing.
I crumble beneath the weight of my own desires,

I am so weary of what I want to be;
How I want others to see me.
I cling to all that I have
With the crazed hunger of a rabid beast.
I fight off anything that dare draw near
To take what I have always known;
What I don't want to change.
And yet,
I see the dancing of vibrant colors on the horizon
Tempting me to release what I hold with such
    ferocious intensity,
To leave it all behind and start afresh.
I tiptoe around the pain
That lies in shards upon the shadowy ground.
I listen to the hollow footsteps that are my own
As I peer around each corner
Only to see white walls and empty corridors.
I glance behind me.
Bloody footprints;
They follow me wherever I go.
Why is there pain
In the blank spaces?
Where did the color go?
Why are my tears visiting me in the silence?
There.
I see something.

Color. Buckets of color. Brushes. Paint brushes.
The white walls surround me on every side,
They swallow me with their bleak emptiness,
They scream at me in the silence.
With a trembling hand,
I grasp a paint brush
And begin to paint.
It is here that I learn many things.
Here in the halls of time,
In the waiting,
In the shards of my hurt,
I learn to paint away the grey, the white, the sadness.
Here in the silence,
I learn to speak
To pray when the quiet air pushes me, suffocates
   me, bullies me.
Here in the blank spaces,
In the halls of my darkened memories,
I learn to dance with my pain,
To grab it by its black claws
And lead it in a waltz through the echoey hallways.
I will remember these dark and silent days,
These days of blankness and monotony.
For without the darkness,
I would not know light.
Without the grey,

I would not know color.
Without the silence,
I would not know music.
Without the pain,
I would not know joy.
I will paint my passions upon the blank walls of
  my loneliness,
I will twirl with the hurt that tries to keep me
  captive,
I will sing into the silence until my heart dances
  with the melody.
The clock is ticking,
Ticking,
Ticking,
And it cannot be stopped.
But as I stand here in the blank spaces,
There is a shadow I rest in;
Not the shadow of an intruder,
But the shadow of One who has brought me here.
I will dwell in His comfort
As I sing and dance and paint joy
Into every blank space.

CLOSER

I don't always feel Your hand in mine,
But I know You are guiding me
As I put one trembling foot in front of the other.
I will jump from stone to stone
As I cross this raging river of life,
Knowing that each leap
Is one leap closer to being in Your presence.

YOU LOVE ME

You love me.
How could I doubt this?
I cry in the night,
Drenching my pillow with my
Sorrows and frustrations,
Allowing my mind to erupt
With depressing, destructive thoughts
Instead of calling out to You.
You love me.
And yet I push Your love away
As I try to make sense
Of my pain,
Forgetting that You ordain everything
In Your perfect wisdom.
You love me.
Until I believe it in my heart
Instead of just knowing it in my head,
I will declare this
Again and again
As I look to the cross
And bury myself in Your Word.
You love me.
Even when darkness tries to smother all light,

You Love Me

When truth and hope are muted
By the wails of despair and confusion,
Your love descends upon me
In a cascading avalanche of affection.
You love me.
When I feel trampled by rejection,
As I search for love and acceptance,
You remind me that You delight in me,
That You held my heart before anyone—
That You are my first love.
You love me.
Your love often comes in forms
That I do not receive immediately.
I run away from it
When it causes me to feel pain,
Even though I know it is a mercy.
You love me.
How can I question this truth
When You became sin for me,
So I would not suffer the punishment
I deserve?
Your sacrifice and brutal death
Were the very embodiment of love.
You love me.
Your pierced hands cradle the heart
That You died for.

My heart.
In You, I will never be unloved.
You don't just pour out these affections,
You are love.
You love me.
Your affections do not retreat from me
When I fail You,
Or bring shame upon myself.
You gently correct me,
And yet Your love for me
Does not flicker for a moment.
You love me.
Every step I take,
Every tear I shed,
Encapsulates Your love and goodness.
For everything in my life
Is according to Your perfect plan
  and purpose.

PURSUER

With darkness as my outer cloak,
I hid myself in shadows deep,
With muffled steps and bated breath,
I left a town possessed with sleep.

Creeping to the ground like fog,
I weaved between both vines and trees,
Aware, and silent as the grave,
I heard and felt the icy breeze.

Always running, always fleeing,
Gripping terror real as pain,
Kept me going, kept me breathless,
Pumping, surging through each vein.

Blending, melting in the dark,
I hid in caves no man could find,
But still my panicked heart declared
That someone still pursued behind.

Climbing mountains in the night,
Descending hills and rocky peaks,
Slipping through the trees and woods,
Crossing rivers, streams, and creeks.

I sought a place to simply hide,
I tried to flee and get away.
The anguish and the bitter guilt
Had rooted fast and come to stay.

But still I floundered in despair,
With desperate haste I stumbled on.
I dared to hope, I dared to trust
That my pursuer now had gone.

Panting hard with bleeding feet,
I tried to leave it all behind.
The searing memories, deep and real,
Would never leave my racing mind.

So desperate now, I did the worst:
I neared the beach with sand of gold,
And looking out with hands clenched tight,
I neared the water, deep and cold.

To cast myself upon the waves,
To swim beneath the ocean's tide,
Became my only option then,
My only place to truly hide.

I had stumbled; fled with fear,
Through forests, fields, and caves abroad,

Pursuer

The only goal upon my heart,
Was fleeing from the One called God.

But as I stepped into the sea,
And as the water chilled my skin,
I knew no matter what I tried,
I'd never hide, I'd never win.

And if I flew above the earth,
And entered heaven in the sky,
The Lord would surely be up there,
Just waiting as I passed Him by.

And if I made my bed in hell,
The King of kings would be there too.
And if with wings, I took to flight,
He'd watch me fly through skies of blue.

No pocket in the universe
Could blot me from the Savior's sight,
Could make my sins become unseen,
Or hide my failures in the night.

And if I killed my wicked soul,
And perished in a hidden place,
The Lord would watch me die in sin,
He'd watch the life drain from my face.

So as I stood upon the beach,
Surrounded by the sea and wind,
With coldness creeping in my bones,
I wished that I had never sinned.

But then a thought invaded me;
It probed my mind and stirred my soul.
And as I watched the darkened sky,
I wondered at my only goal.

Was hiding, running, always fleeing,
Helping me with life's despair?
I let the question burrow deep,
As salty winds blew through the air.

And as I gazed upon the sea,
The black horizon still in sight,
A distant color glowed with warmth,
And penetrated in the night.

A tingle traveled up my spine,
As beams of light exploded high.
The heavens brimmed with radiance,
As colors danced across the sky.

The icy chill began to melt,
The inky shadows disappeared,

Pursuer

And as I stared at blazing light,
I heard His voice, the one I feared.

It roared, it shook the very ground,
It rumbled in a booming shout,
With power deep and power wide,
He let His words spill forth and spout.

"You thought that you could hide from Me,
You tried to cover up your sin.
You sought for refuge in the dark,
And thought that you would surely win.

"But you can never run from Me,
The darkness will not be your friend.
Destruction and complete defeat
Will only follow in the end.

"The more you run, the more you hide,
The more you flee in violent fear,
The closer I will be to you,
The more I'll follow and draw near.

"But if you stop and if you turn,
And if you let me see your face,
And if you run into My arms,
Then I will surely give you grace.

"For hiding will not give you peace,
And fleeing will not give you life.
The sin will only come to stay,
And tear and rip you like a knife.

"So listen to My voice and heed
That if you run, I'll still pursue.
But if you trust Me and repent,
Then I will give My grace to you."

Something burst inside my heart;
I threw myself into the sand.
I let the darkness fall away,
And raised my arm, my shaking hand.

I then revealed myself to Him,
I let Him see my wounds and scars.
I watched His light engulf the dark
As nighttime faded with the stars.

The great pursuer, He had won,
My rotting soul collapsed and died.
I stood there, new and now revealed,
Without a single thing to hide.

COFFIN OF LIES

I walk through dark passageways,
Swatting at the cobwebs of monotony,
Treading through puddles of mundane living.
Depression does not cloak me,
And yet joy is a far-off friend;
A mere dot on my cloudy horizon.
I cannot see to the right or to the left;
The dim light in front of me
Flickers faintly at the end of this tunnel.
And then it happens.
The hollow walls on either side of me
Splinter into a thousand pieces,
Ripped from the floor and whisked into the
    swirling air,
Like the walls of a mere dollhouse.
The cobwebs vanish in the blinding light.
The puddles explode into one babbling,
    rushing brook.
My static heart begins to pulse with life
As a soft wind caresses my face.
The stars blink down on me with innocence,
And the velvet sky softens to a pale pink
As the rising sun peeks over the hillside.

Flowers the color of honey
Glisten against the green foliage that carpets
    the ground.
My first thought is:
Why could all of this not have been present
    in my life before?
But then I look at the carnage around me —
The blackened maze of my own misery,
And realize that I had cloaked
What had been there all along.
I had constructed a coffin
Around my own heart,
As the Lord's mercies blossomed around me,
Forgotten, ignored, and despised
By the heart barely pulsing within
A casket of selfishness.
May the beauty of my Savior
Penetrate the walls of monotony
That I so often build with my own hands,
And may joy be an ever-present companion
    in every waking moment.

THE LONELY ROAD

Those who may not
Have friends for a season,
Who are greeted by silence
Each morning
And wander the empty
Halls of their minds;
Those who sit beside
The still waters of grief
And amble down the road of suffering
With a burden on their shoulders;
Who walk the vast emptiness
Of a barren wasteland
And watch the cloudless sky
With expectant eyes;
Those who shed tears in secret
And wonder
Why the pain burns their heart
Like a consuming fire;
Who long to walk with light steps
And wish to find consolation
In the presence of others —
Can there be found
Such depth,

Such passion,
Such wisdom,
Such discernment,
Such empathy,
In anyone but
Those who have faced these waves of trouble?
They have wandered the wilderness
And found the heart of God.
They have plunged into its depths,
Tasted of its sweetness,
And clung to Him whom they treasure
More than anything this world can offer.
This lonely path
Is the most sacred one,
For though the ache may be great,
There is more room for Him who satisfies,
And His presence is a never-ending chasm
Of deep, lasting, incomprehensible joy.

MY GREATEST TREASURE

I minimize Your love for me
When I compare myself to others
And assume You have given them better gifts.
I reduce Your goodness to ashes
When I loathe my pain
And wonder if there is any purpose in it.
I allow Your might and power
To become small in my mind
When I don't trust
My future in Your hands.
Your nearness is made far and distant
In my heart,
When I allow fear to rob me
Of my joy.
I treat Your comfort as worthless
When I embrace depression
And succumb to my anxieties.
I question Your omniscience
When I complain about my circumstances,
And am discontent with the season of life
   You have placed me in.
I throw Your compassion to the wind
When I run to others for consolation

Instead of You.
I take Your patience for granted
When I come to You for forgiveness
Again and again,
And don't see Your mercy
As a marvelous thing.
I disrespect Your holiness
When I only worship You in church,
And hardly think of You throughout the week.
I act as if grace doesn't exist
When I forget about the cross
And what You did for a wretch like me.
Your sovereignty becomes an afterthought
When I worry about tomorrow
And allow my fears to consume me.
I give Your truth away willingly
When I allow the lies of the world
To take root in my mind.
I reject the peace You offer me
When I drown myself in my duties
And refuse to rest in You.
I challenge Your wisdom
When I am angry at You
For not giving me what I desire.
I act as if I despise Your company
When my prayers are silent

My Greatest Treasure

And my Bible lies untouched
Beside my bed.
You have given me a chest
Overflowing with priceless treasures,
And I leave it in a dark corner
As it collects dust.
I fill myself with everything
But You,
And You are the greatest gift of all.
I can declare to the world
My love for You all I want,
But if I don't receive the glorious attributes
　You offer me,
My words are merely ashes in my mouth
That mean nothing.
Help me to treat You as my greatest treasure,
For that is what You are.

UNCAGED

My feelings, my passions,
The very essence of who I am,
Reside inside me,
Like delicate birds in a cage.
They are locked in this prison,
"To be kept safe,"
I tell myself.
I fear that they will be harmed,
Thrown away, mistreated, or lost altogether
If I set them free.
But I must ask myself one question:
Is avoiding risk
Worth keeping the embodiment of myself
Locked away
To wither in the darkness?
These restless cares and feelings may be safe
From rejection,
But they will never see the light of day,
Feel the wind in their wings,
Nor soar into the clouds
Where they will meet joy and freedom.
Unlock this cage, my friend.
There is beauty in risk,

Uncaged

For caution that is rooted in fear
Holds hands with Isolation himself.
God did not mold you
So that you could hide yourself
Away from the world.
Release the essence of yourself
To be used for God's glory,
For though the heavens
May swallow you in their enormity,
You will always be engulfed in His presence.
That is freedom.

IF YOU HAD NOT...

If You had not allowed me to suffer,
I would not have cast myself into Your arms.
If You had not stripped me of earthly treasures,
I would have been too full to seek for Your love.
If You had not shown me sorrow,
I would not have treasured Your comfort.
If You had not taken away what I loved,
I would not have filled my heart with more of You.
If You had not allowed me to wait,
I would not have been strengthened and matured
    by patience.
If You had not allowed my heart to break,
I would not have known the depth of
    tearful prayers.
If You had not allowed my struggles to persist,
I would be shallow, undiscerning, and self-serving.
If You had not shown me trials,
I would not have been able to comfort others.
If You had not made me empty,
I would not have known what it meant to be
    satisfied in You.

HE WILL FIND YOU

Sit in the puddles of your sadness,
Let the cold raindrops
Cover your drooping form
In soaking sheets of gloom.
The pain will always be there
Whether you sit in it
Or run from its
Tangled arms of blackness.
And yet—
If you let it pass over you,
If you give in to its crushing embrace
You will feel the embrace of another.
His arms will enfold you
As the torrents of pain
Lash at you like a whip.
But oh, the healing that will encompass you
As you cling to the Healer
Who sent the storm you are weathering.
Let the tears come,
Sit in the shadows
Until His sweet song finds you
With deep notes of comfort.

THE BRIDGE TO SAVING GRACE

I trembled when I thought of You,
For Your being seemed a million miles away,
And yet Your wrath crouched near,
As I felt its hot breath on my face.
My sins reached to the heavens
Like a monstrous mountain of darkness,
Hiding Your face from me,
Casting a shadow of death on my quaking form.
A chasm stood between us;
An abyss I had created and dug
With my own folly.
All was hopelessly lost
Until that dark day,
When lightning cracked the sky into fragments,
And a throng of voices screamed in
Agony, rage, and mockery.
A multitude watched
As a man hung from a cross of wood.
His words rang through the air:
"It is finished."
It was then
That an impenetrable veil
Was rent from top to bottom.

The Bridge to Saving Grace

Never before had this veil
Been cast aside,
For no one had been granted access
To the Father.
I now stand at the edge of my chasm,
Staring in awe and wonder
At a bridge
That now stretches from one side
To the other.
I tremble as I set one foot
On its surface
And allow myself to stand
With my full weight upon it.
I look over to the other side of the abyss,
Where I know You are waiting.
Suddenly, I am not afraid.
I know that Your wrath
Has already been satisfied.
Although I am unworthy,
I know that if I leave my mountain
Of sin behind me,
And give my heart to You,
I will be clean.
You beckon me with Your love,
As a father beckons his child.
All at once, I am running.

All Things Broken & Beautiful

Tears sting my eyes
As the solid bridge beneath my feet
Guides me to the other side.
Your presence is no longer
Shrouded by the veil of my sin,
For the wooden cross
Became a bridge
That made it possible for me
To run into Your presence.

TRAGEDY

It seems a tragedy
That I will never love You
As much as You love me.
My heart breaks
As my speck of love
Is lost in the ocean that is Yours.
It truly is a wonder
That I can never span
Or measure
The depth of Your affection.
As I drown in its enormity,
I suddenly realize
That my fragility is beautiful
As Your strength encompasses it.
I was never meant
To match Your love,
For You, my King
Are matchless.

I NEEDED MORE OF HIM

You love my heart so deeply
That you claim it as Your own.
You strip me of my idols
So there's room for You alone.
You give my pain permission
To help me grow and learn.
You bring me to the desert,
So there's nowhere else to turn.
You will not ever share me;
You're jealous and You're kind.
You want to fill my everything—
My soul, my heart, my mind.
Though I may fight and question You,
Your patience never wanes.
You are my light, my comforter,
My shelter when it rains.
You see my weak and wretched state,
And yet You love me still.
Though I may stumble, fall, and fail,
I know You never will.
You take my bleeding, fractured heart,
You fill it to the brim,
So I can tell each passerby,
"I needed more of Him!"

DRAW ME

To think that all my fears and worries
Never once touch my future
Or change what will come to pass.
To think that my anxiety
Only distances me from my Father
And mars the joy that could be.
To think that when I am afraid,
My heart believes lies,
And the thorns of doubt begin to creep
Into my heart.
Lord, help me to hide behind
A shield of trust,
To throw my fears to the wind
And bask in the grace You have for me today.
Draw me to You,
As the tide is drawn to the shore,
As a moth is drawn to light,
As a bee is drawn to a flower.
Human beings are drawn
To what fills them with awe.
They are drawn to treasure,
But why do they so often gravitate toward
    everything
But You?

HIS GREATEST WARRIORS

Despair is like an iron hand,
As it destroys every breath of hope in my body.
Fear, its right-hand man,
Whispers in my ear,
Telling me that all will be well.
I succumb to its beckoning;
Discontentment settles over loaded blessings,
Like a layer of dust,
Masking every glimmer of beauty.
Selfishness blocks out everything
Except my own reflection,
Causing me to ignore the needs of others.
And yet, when Hope steals softly in the room,
They all freeze in terror,
And pause in the midst of their destruction.
Just a few steps behind comes Joy,
Illuminating the place with its blinding light.
Quaking in terror, the rest of them
Are not prepared for the last deadly blow.
Love comes pouring in from every side like water,
Flooding out every last trace of filth and darkness.

Part Three

THE MENDING

MENDER

I often wander the dark recesses of my mind,
And curl up in a corner,
Waiting.
What do I wait for?
It often changes.
Sometimes I wait for my pain to ebb and melt away,
Like a candle that burns and burns.
Maybe the pain will burn for so long that it'll melt
Into a cold, hard mass of nothingness.
Feeling nothing may be better than crumbling
Beneath the hurt that pierces my soul.
Sometimes I wait for Joy.
I listen for its sweet melody;
I search for it in the inky blackness.
I also wait for Truth to come storming through the
    walls that cage me in,
To hold me close and fight off the lies that
Tear at me like ravenous wolves.
At times I wander from this dark recess
And peek through the doors of my eyes.
I watch people pass me by,
Knowing that they too are looking through doors
    that lead to dark places.

I am thankful that I don't stay here.
For Joy and Truth do indeed come,
And they bring with them another friend.
His name is Hope.
They carry me with gentle arms
And lay me at the feet of the One who sent them.
That is where I stay.
I kneel there, knowing that all I needed to do
    was come
And offer up the fractured pieces of my heart
With trembling hands
That can no longer bear this burden.
Here is where I wait,
As my Father takes my wounded heart
And mends it with skillful hands.
For it is He who knows it best.
How can I be afraid when I have returned my heart
To the One who created it?
I don't rush Him,
For I know it will be restored in His timing,
And will be stronger and more beautiful than
    ever before.
So here I wait,
Sitting quietly,
Enjoying the presence of my Mender.

NEVER ABANDONED

The ugly, horrific things of this world,
Are wiped away in an instant
By your glory and splendor.
Help me to see You
In every droplet and puddle,
In each sunset
And breath of wind.
You are glorious,
You are Sweet,
You are everything.
Thank You for carrying me
And giving me strength
When I felt glued to my bed,
And my body was heavy with sorrow.
Thank You for clearing my mind
And giving me energy,
When anxiety clouded every thought,
And fatigue riddled my limbs.
Thank You for giving me life
Through Your word,
And calming my fears
With Your presence.
Help me remember

All Things Broken & Beautiful

That the fingers of grace have
Never unwrapped themselves
From my heart,
And Your very Spirit
Dwells within it.
I shall never be abandoned.

ARROWS

I have spent my life waiting,
Wondering,
Striving,
Wishing.
And yet God has quieted my restless soul
By piercing me with His love.
At first the force of it was too much to bear,
And I thought that I was mortally wounded;
I cried out in fear and panic.
I did not know
That sometimes
His love is found
In the darkest of times.
Like an arrow to the heart,
The moment it hits its mark
Is horribly painful.
I stagger beneath the excruciating agony
And call out for help.
Moments stretch into hours,
And hours into days,
As I suffer through this pain.
It isn't until more time has passed
That I realize
This arrow has been dipped

In the sweet balm of God's abounding love
And its healing power
Is spreading through my entire being.
In the midst of my wishing,
And the restlessness of my soul,
He has pinned me under His love
So I will not go astray.
Suddenly,
The shaft breaks to pieces;
The arrowhead falls to the ground.
I push myself to my feet
Looking down at the fractured arrow.
My heart has been scarred
With pain and sorrow,
And yet God has left His mark on me.
He is the bowman
And I am His target.
A love like this,
A love so fierce,
So direct,
So purposeful,
So transforming,
Can be found nowhere else.
This arrow has brought me agony;
And yet, it has brought me God Himself.
It has invaded my heart
And has made it whole.

TIME

Time is a thief,
A merciless enemy that pulls me through space,
Like a corpse being dragged
Behind a speeding vehicle.
I want to breathe,
To pause for just a moment,
To freeze the moving pictures,
The blur of colors parading by
Like a circus of chaos and spiraling memories.
Why does fear clutch me by the throat
And taunt me of all I have not yet accomplished?
I weep into the chasm of lost years,
I grasp at the shards of all that once was.
I'm not ready to leave it all behind,
To become frail beneath the weight of the world.
Did I love enough?
Did I clothe myself with joy,
When the cloak of sadness threatened to drown
    me in darkness?
Did I pause to savor life's beauty?
Did I live for that which I will never lose?
Maybe time is not a thief,
But a healer,
A gentle rain that waters a withered soul,

And puts out a thousand fires.
Time whispers to pain,
Coaxing it to another land,
While ushering in
A sweet harvest of healing.
Perhaps time
Is a gracious friend,
A listening ear
In the putrid pit of sorrow,
When light seems an impossibility.
Time smoothes out the wrinkles of despair,
It blankets us with a forgetfulness
That brings startling relief.
Without time,
I would live a thousand sorrows
In a frozen state of agony.
Without time,
My youth would bind me
In a prison of stunted growth.
Time has carried me to the tallest mountain,
Turned my sapling into a tree of abundance,
Ushered me deeper and deeper
Into the greatest love I've ever known.
Time is not my enemy,
But one of God's greatest mercies.

CRAFTSMAN

I wrestle with darkness
And flee the jagged shards of pain,
As I desperately try to gather up
The shattered pieces of my heart.
I am trying to become my own mender.
I know it is hopeless and vain
To even attempt this;
The fragments of my heart
Slip through my fingers
As I search for relief in the shadows,
And wade through the lake that is my tears.
Your voice beckons me in the midst of my search.
You draw me away from my pitiful groping,
You tell me that I am trying to do
What cannot be done.
I sit at Your feet
With bones too weary to move
And eyes too heavy to fix upward.
My head is bent
As if a weighted chain
Hangs about my neck.
You do not reprimand me,
Nor do You shame me

As I sit there, soaked and forlorn;
A fragile, helpless mess.
You don't say anything at all,
But instead,
You take off Your thick, glorious cloak,
And wrap it securely around
My shivering form.
I settle into its warmth
As safety and security
Fill my being,
As loneliness and pain
Begin to retreat.
You get up from Your seat,
Letting me sit there,
Safely wrapped in the warmest coat
I have ever worn,
And You begin to gather the pieces of my heart
That are still scattered in the shadows.
I marvel at the effortless ease
With which You go about it,
For it had been an impossible task for me.
But even as I watch,
I begin to relax as I sit engulfed in Your cloak,
As its soothing warmth overtakes my being,
And I slip into a world of soft relief.
I suddenly jolt awake,

Craftsman

Realizing I had fallen asleep,
Not knowing how or when
It had happened.
You are now sitting before me,
And when I behold Your gaze
And feel the wholeness within me,
I know what has transpired.
Wrapped in Your cloak of Comfort,
My turmoil had been put to rest,
And all the while,
You, the Craftsman of my heart,
Had been mending
What I could not mend myself.

EXCRUCIATING LOVE

With every sunrise,
I am reminded of the empty tomb
On that glorious third day,
When the very air was thick with sorrow
And all hope was merely a passing vapor.
The barren cross was stained with blood
And stood upon the hill
As an eerie reminder of the horror that had
    taken place just days before.
To think that You thought of me
As the iron nails pinned You there,
And Your shredded body hung above
The mass of chaos, mockery, and hysteria.
The world saw a man suffering
At the hands of wicked men,
But they only glimpsed a fraction of Your
    indescribable pain.
For God had ripped back the heavens
And poured His wrath on His own Son
In an onslaught of excruciating love.
Each day,
I am enfolded by grace on every side,
Provided by the very blood shed for me that day.

I am living a life completely undeserved,
And yet I will never have to pay for it.
It has already been paid for;
My sins have been disintegrated, abolished,
   obliterated.
May I daily remember
Your crimson blood,
The splintered cross on the hill,
And the empty tomb.
They are not distant symbols,
But have left a permanent mark on me.
I will never be the same.

FLAMING NIGHT

Swaying grass, silky skirt,
Gentle footsteps in the dirt,
Windy whispers, blackest night,
Open meadow, calming sight.
Tousled curls, shining eyes,
Sprinkled stars on charcoal skies,
Breathless awe, racing heart,
Gaping at God's wondrous art.
Skirt soft, wind so sweet,
Summer's glade devoid of heat,
Spinning, dancing, grass so tall,
Darkness thick and stars so small.
Flecks of light begin to rise,
Reflecting stars in blackest skies,
Within the grass, a flaming sea,
Erupting; no apology.
Fireflies, their light aflame,
Chase each other in their game,
First up high and then down low,
Dancing where they want to go.
Blackened night, a shining glade,
Rippling grass, an orange shade,
Peaceful place devoid of day,
Where fireflies come out to play.

ORDINARY THINGS

When I find joy in the little things,
My life becomes
A collection of colorful snapshots
That I tuck away,
In a scrapbook of vivid artistry.
Each page
Makes me see the world
As a larger puzzle
Made up of small seemingly insignificant pieces.
As I see its exhilarating beauty,
My heart is soon captured by ordinary things.
Raindrops racing down my window,
The smell of fresh, new books,
The softness of a puppy's fur,
And the wetness of its kisses on my cheek.
Gleeful chatter throughout the house,
Clattering sounds from the kitchen
As a delicious breakfast is being made.
Golden sunbeams dancing on the walls
And illuminating each room.
Patches of the pastel blue sky
Scattered in the heavens
Like a brightly-colored quilt of comfort.

All Things Broken & Beautiful

A picnic on the front lawn,
Accompanied by fun pastimes, such as
Drawing, reading, making music,
And inventing new games.
The chirping of birds in the trees,
Who are naive to a troubled world,
And sing to their heart's content.
The vibrant flowers
That cling to vines
As they cover fences
Like a multi-colored blanket.
Morning coffee,
Warming me up,
And filling the house
With a rich aroma.
Quiet moments in the backyard,
Spent with my Savior
As I meditate on His Word.
Life itself is a wondrous thing,
Bursting with beauty at every turn.
Sometimes it takes a restful pause
To notice that the things we see every day
Are not so ordinary after all.

MY SHIELD

You are oh so kind to me;
Your grace protects me like a shield,
Your mercy floods my heart
Like a rushing stream.
Your love rescues my soul
And sets it high upon the rock of hope.
You bury my fears
In Your promises,
You steady my quaking heart
With Your faithful care.
You guide me through
Darkened paths;
You light my way with Your truth.
You carry me
When I cannot take another step.
You still my being
With Your presence.

NEW EVERY MORNING

Each morning is a fresh page,
Shimmering with dew
And golden sunlight.
The night's wrestling is a distant dream.
The baggage of yesterday
Has been taken care of,
Washed away by the tender waves of grace.
The struggles of the day before
Have been laid to rest.
I accept Your cup of mercy
That You have refilled
And given me for the day.
This is not yesterday's mercy,
Nor is it tomorrow's.
It is for today,
And it is enough.
Though I may face fresh billows of sorrow or pain,
I know that this cup
Will fill me and give me strength
To the day's end.
I can begin today
With a bursting heart of joy,
For You are a good Father,
And Your mercies are new every morning.

FILLED

You load me with blessings
And give me gifts I don't deserve.
I thank You for them,
But set them aside as soon
As I receive them.
I peer into the distance,
Waiting for my next blessing.
My heart's gratitude
Is merely a layer at the surface
That evaporates in moments.
I forget
That if it was not
For Your lovingkindness,
I would be running
Through the gates of hell.
Your salvation alone
Has saved me
From the claws of eternal death.
I wrestle with untethered desire,
I try to throttle the monster
Of discontentment.
I struggle with deep restlessness,
And wonder about what lies ahead.

I crave more;
I demand to be given
Everything that I desire.
And yet,
If I had it all,
Would I ever turn to You?
Would I hide myself in You
When emptiness
Drained me of my joy?
I would never treasure
The greatest gift of all
Which is You.
If my contentment
Finds deep roots in Your presence,
My joy will burst forth in bloom,
And will thrive through every storm.
I will not gaze at the horizon
With anxious eyes
And a wanting heart,
For You fill my soul,
Leaving room for nothing else.

STEADFAST GOODNESS

Despite the way my life should go,
Through every season, ebb, and flow,
Your goodness never goes away,
It's firmly fastened through each day.
The sky may shine with spotless blue,
Or hold a gray and gloomy hue,
My lips may find a joyful song,
Or grow silent before long.
This does not affect His love,
His goodness reigns from up above,
His plans are steadfast, good, and true,
He holds my hand and guides me, too.

GARMENTS OF JOY

Why is it
That joy must always
Be fought for?
Oh, how glorious it will be
When I awake in heaven,
And joy will be my very garments.
For now,
I will wake with the sun,
And search for joy in the shadows,
Knowing that one day
I will awake in the presence
Of the Son Himself.

MY CUP RUNS OVER

I sit at Your table,
And watch as You set a cup before me.
I immediately grasp it
With trembling hands
As my throat burns
And my dry, cracked lips
Beg for relief
From this thirst.
I gulp the sweet contents
Of the golden cup,
And although my thirst
Is quenched momentarily,
I want more
As soon as I lower the cup
To the table.
Hours go by
As I sit at Your table,
Looking with longing eyes
At my empty cup.
My parched mouth is dry and coarse,
My throat screams in pain
As I grasp the cup.
I pick it up

And desperately drain
The last few drops
That have settled in the bottom.
The liquid tickles my throat
With a taunting sweetness,
And my mouth is once again inflamed;
My thirst only increases.
Although I have sat here
For what seems to be an eternity,
I do not know
That You have stood at the table
This whole time.
You watch me suffer
As I lick at the meager droplets,
Longing for relief.
I lift my gaze for the first time
And see You standing there.
You look on me with compassion,
And yet,
You do not refill my cup.
You sit down across from me,
And You listen
As I tell You of my troubles.
You do not condemn me,
Nor do You scoff at me.
You are gentle with me;

My Cup Runs Over

You fill my heart with a hope
That I cannot describe.
You tell me who I am;
You know me better than I know myself.
I am taken aback,
And listen as You pour loving words
Into my soul.
You begin to tell me who You are,
And I am filled with awe
As I behold Your likeness.
You are love,
You are hope,
You are a refuge to confide in.
You are holy,
You are beautiful.
My thirst is forgotten,
And the cup is all
But nonexistent.
My pain subsides
As I soak in Your presence;
I am filled with peace.
Suddenly, my hands on the table
Become drenched
In a cold liquid.
I look down at the table,
And my empty cup,

All Things Broken & Beautiful

Is now overflowing
With a sweet and refreshing drink.
My cup runs over;
It falls with a crash
As the drink
Gushes in abundance.
My eyes fill with tears
As I behold You once again;
Your presence alone
Has produced an overflowing fountain
Of goodness and mercy.
It is more than enough for me.

HIDDEN IN YOU

You are the song of my heart,
The one who stitches up my wounds
With gentle hands.
When my tears burn my cheeks,
And my heart is bruised and battered,
You stay by my side
Through every second of my pain.
When my thoughts tumble about in chaos,
And my emotions rage without order,
You calm the storm of my soul
With just a word.
When fear clutches me in the night,
And doubt whispers poisonous lies in my ear,
You illuminate the darkness,
And cast them into the shadows.
You hear my trembling prayers,
You hide me in Your love,
You guide me through the maze of life,
You make loneliness an impossibility.

HIDING PLACE

Twining flowers, sprawling trees,
Curling vines and buzzing bees,
Velvet grass and babbling streams,
Fading by like pleasant dreams.

Swirling petals in the breeze,
Salty wind from distant seas,
Puffy clouds against the sky,
Pass the birds that swoop and fly.

Colors dancing in the sun,
Sunlight gleaming as I run
Through the meadow, through the glade,
Through the beech trees' soothing shade.

Dashing, splashing, dancing, spinning,
Racing deer and never winning,
Sending dew drops through the air,
Throwing leaves without a care.

Little sparrows' melodies
Floating down from apple trees,
Rabbits leaping, owls nesting,
Foxes prancing, badgers resting.

Hiding Place

I can hear the wind that sighs,
I can see the butterflies,
I can feel the sun and breeze,
I can smell the cherry trees.

But I can't stop to watch and look,
I run while clinging to a book,
I run as if I'm in a race
To find a certain, secret place.

Dodging, stumbling, ducking, leaping,
Through the briars, always creeping,
Heading for the distant creek,
I near the secret place I seek.

Maple trees with leaves aflame
Bending without any shame,
Give me shelter, give me shade,
As I scamper through the glade.

Barefoot, tramping through the leaves
Gazing up at hanging eaves,
Hugging close the sacred book,
I listen to the nearing brook.

Winding paths and bending lanes,
Beaten down by storms and rains,

Lead me on as sunlight shimmers
Through the trees with golden glimmers.

Faster, faster, almost there,
Gusts of wind blow through my hair,
Tripping, stumbling, nearly falling,
I can hear my river calling.

Following the path ahead
Wreathed with leaves the trees had shed,
I turn the corner, round the bend,
And race ahead to see my Friend.

Trees with leaves of flaming red
Have their branches fully spread
Over trees with leaves of green,
Hiding what has not been seen.

But I can see it, only I,
Now I run there, now I fly,
Excitement bubbles up inside,
As I dash to what I've spied.

I halt, I stop and tilt my head,
I gaze with wonder up ahead,
I hear the water down below,
Trickling at a steady flow.

Hiding Place

A bridge with arches made of stone,
On the river, all alone,
Makes a path across the stream,
Still and peaceful, like a dream.

The river, swirling green and blue,
Whispers, laughs, and babbles too,
As I cross the bridge of stone,
Knowing that I'm not alone.

Stopping there with eyes closed tight,
I clutch the book with all my might,
I let the wind caress my face,
In the earth's most secret place.

Safe from troubles, safe from war,
Safe from grief that eats my core,
Safe from people, safe from pain,
Safe from storms and gloom and rain.

The solid bridge beneath my feet,
The fragrant breeze, so soft and sweet,
The vibrant trees, surrounding me,
Warm my heart and set me free.

But all around, amongst the leaves,
Up above, beyond the eaves,

Someone lives there, watching me
Someone there Who I can't see.

This place, so peaceful and serene,
With leaves of red and leaves of green,
Isn't where I've come to hide,
Isn't where my bonds are tied.

Someone mighty, Someone strong,
Someone who has done no wrong,
Someone full of peace and grace
Has always been my hiding place.

Fingering the precious book,
I flip a page, and peer to look,
I read a bit, then close my eyes
And stand there as the hour flies.

Light is fading from the day,
But still I meditate and pray,
Wind is blowing from the West,
But still I stay to think and rest.

Surrounded by His love and grace,
I cannot leave this peaceful place,
Filled with joy and filled with praise,
I could stay here all my days.

Hiding Place

In the presence of my King,
I can praise Him, I can sing,
But here, it's easiest of all,
Though anywhere, He'll hear my call.

Vivid colors, laughing stream,
Peaceful like a pleasant dream,
Savior's presence, joyful praise,
A God Who's with me all my days.

Someone mighty, Someone strong,
Someone who has done no wrong,
Someone full of peace and grace
Has always been my hiding place.

LOVE IS AGONY

Sometimes I wish love was a fantasy,
A mirage that vanished when the sun sets,
A lamp that can be switched off in an instant.
But here I am
With its stains on my skin
In permanent ink.
I try to tear at the pulsing mass in my chest,
But this volcano of pain and affection
Cannot be extinguished.
To love is to be in agony.
When the tattered pages of time
Fly in the wind,
The deeper the pain reaches with its
    frigid fingers.
Love is a ravaging storm,
A wildfire,
A gentle wind.
Love is not meant for one person
But for enough faces and hearts
To fill a book.
To love is to pour into countless vessels,
Only to find that the heart becomes fuller
With each offering.

How can one heart be this full without bursting?
To love is to feel loss,
To love is to fall into the arms of loneliness,
To grasp the air for what once was.
But perhaps love is all things beautiful,
Perhaps it is why life pulses within me,
Why I wake up each day
And push the heavy covers off my broken self.
To love is to keep a record of names locked away,
To look at someone and feel a tightness,
A clenching in the soul.
To love is to feel the sting of tears,
A sudden avalanche in every crevice,
A rushing of a thousand waterfalls.
To love is to crumble
At the thought of seeing a face for the last time.
To love is to weep over
The childhood pictures
Of one who is no longer a child.
To love is to not know whether
To laugh or cry,
Whether to run toward or away.
Perhaps love is the air we breathe,
The sun that peeks at us through our foggy windows.
Love is why we exist,
For He who is Love

Holds the universe together.
To love is to gain and to lose,
To weep and to laugh,
To know wild joy and debilitating pain.
Who can measure the vastness of the heart?
Such a small lump of flesh,
And yet its walls can hold multitudes.
If pain and love must coexist together
Then so be it,
For though it may be unbearable at times,
At least life is pulsing from within.

THE THRESHOLD OF HEAVEN

Sometimes I feel it breathing on my face;
It is a sweet aroma,
And yet oftentimes it's a stench.
Is that my own casket that I smell?
I can hear the funeral march of my heart pumping
Before it ceases forever.
I also smell the sweet breath of wind
That caresses my face through the open
Doorway of heaven.
How horrifyingly beautiful it is
That when my fleshly carcass
Is enveloped by the earth,
My new body, whole and complete,
Will embrace the One who fashioned it.
A sickening departure
Immediately followed by a glorious arrival.
What will I say to Him?
How will I be able to meet His gaze?
Will my breath catch in my throat
When I see the splendors of heaven?
Or will I only see His face?
The darkness of my heart
Cloaks me in its heavy folds

But the hope of heaven
Snuffs out the blackness
As I gaze at the blazing glory
Through the doorway that I have not yet
    entered.
I tremble on its threshold
As this sinful world
Tries to rip me back into its arms
With its painful claws.
I will not be moved from where I stand,
Listening for a whisper of His voice,
Straining for a glimpse of Him
As I wait to be beckoned
Through the door of heaven.
All of life's horrors,
The bleak days of nothingness,
The sharp pangs of hurt,
The loneliness that threatens to choke me,
Will fade to nothing
In the light of this doorway
That floods me with hope and peace.
Oh, to be welcomed
Into the arms of Him who loves me most,
To be held by the Savior
Who was swallowed by death for me.
I know you have not called me home,

The Threshold of Heaven

But here I will wait
On the threshold of heaven
Until that day comes.

IN THE SHADOWS

I fear the darkness in my room,
The tendrils of pain that lurk in the shadows;
The lies that know my name.
I fear what I may find in the stillness,
What my mind may tell me
When the joy of the day has faded.
I fear the great vastness of all that is not known,
The poisoned whispers that cling to my windows
Like cobwebs that cannot be destroyed.
I fear my own reflection,
The weakness that stares back at me through
    vacant eyes,
The sadness that frames my face.
I fear what my heart may say
When I look over my shoulder to the past,
When I see all I've done and haven't done.
I fear the emptiness after a day of fullness,
The quiet after the noise,
The bleak nothingness of my life compared
    to others.
I fear all that I've lost,
All that I once loved
And will never love again.

In the Shadows

I fear what may come,
What may destroy my confidence
And send me to the shadows of my shame.
But as I climb these creaky steps,
I know that in the darkness,
You are there.
I know that when the silence shrouds me,
Your voice encompasses it
In all its glory and power.
I know when I look to the future,
You have already made a place for me,
And Your love guides my way like a beacon in
    the night.
I know that when the lies peek through
    my windows,
You are blowing them away
With a mighty wind that cannot be withstood.
I know that when my mind takes me captive,
You are breaking my shackles
That I may walk in Your freedom.
I know that no shadow can encompass You,
No monster of doubt can stand in Your presence,
No fear can touch the light of who You are.
As I walk into the shadows,
As I step into this darkness,
I know that You are already there.

ALL THINGS BROKEN
AND BEAUTIFUL

Who am I becoming?
I'm frail beneath all that is weary,
I'm distant from my pain,
Detached from a love I once felt.
The inner workings of my heart are
   always changing.
Am I broken or am I strong?
Am I tender or am I numb?
He binds up the broken-hearted,
But what if I never stop breaking?
How many times can a flower's stem
Be bent and snapped in two?
The petals of my joy have fallen,
Have gathered about me
In wilted heaps of defeat.
It is only in the soft hours of silence,
In the pause between songs,
In the haunting lull when the
   darkness comes,
That all is made right.
The replanting of a forgotten bloom,
The mending of a flower,

All Things Broken and Beautiful

As new buds of joy spring forth.
All that once left ghastly wounds
Now only leaves light bruises
That fade as quickly as they appear.
Perhaps I am
All things broken and beautiful,
All things lost and found.
I will not pretend
That my stem is unbreakable,
That my petals will never fall.
But my roots grow deep
In the soil of His goodness,
And I shall not be crushed.
All things broken and beautiful
Grow here,
And I am one of them.